The FIRST BOOK of
MEASUREMENT

The FIRST BOOK of
MEASUREMENT

by SAM and BERYL EPSTEIN

Pictures by Walter Buehr

FRANKLIN WATTS, INC.
575 LEXINGTON AVENUE • NEW YORK 22

7

Library of Congress Catalog Card Number: 60-9788
© Copyright 1960 Franklin Watts, Inc.
Printed in the United States of America
by Polygraphic Company of America, Inc.

CONTENTS

A Special Language

How big is your boat?
How fast does the jet plane go?
How powerful is the rocket's thrust?
How much do you weigh?
You probably hear dozens of questions like this every day — questions that begin with *how big?* or *how fast?* or *how powerful?* or *how much?*

1

Every question like that can be answered in two ways.

Let's say you have a new boat and a friend asks you how big it is. You could answer him in one way by saying, "It's not very big." You are telling the truth, but your friend can't be sure what you mean by "not very big," so he still doesn't know the size of your boat.

The second way to answer the question would be to say, "It's nine feet long."

If you answer the question that way, your friend can be sure of what you mean. You have told him how long your boat is.

Whenever you answer a question that way, you are using a special sort of language called the language of measurement. It is a very useful language, because you can use it to say exactly what you mean, in a way that other people are sure to understand.

Many people use this special language of measurement every day.

If a test pilot takes up a new jet plane on a trial flight, he doesn't write in his report, "The plane went pretty high and traveled very fast." He knows that other people might not understand how high he meant by "pretty high," or how fast by "very fast." Instead he uses the language of measurement and writes, for example, that the plane flew 25,500 feet above the earth at a speed of 520 miles an hour. Then he is certain that everybody who reads his report will know exactly how high and how fast the plane went.

A housewife uses the language of measurement to order exactly what she wants from a store. She doesn't say she wants some cheese and eggs, some good rich milk, and a long piece of clothesline. Instead she orders a pound of cheese, a dozen eggs, a quart of Grade A milk, and 20 yards of clothesline. When she gives a friend a recipe for fudge, she doesn't tell her to use some sugar, milk, corn

2

syrup, chocolate, butter, and vanilla. She uses the language of measurement and tells her to use 2 cups of sugar, ¾ cup of milk, 2 tablespoons of corn syrup, 2 squares, or ounces of chocolate, 3 tablespoons of butter, and 1 teaspoon of vanilla.

Athletes use the language of measurement to keep a record of the time of a race, the height of a pole vault, and the distance covered on a football play.

Engineer drawing plans, using slide rule, T-square, measuring scale, and drawing compass.

Engineers and construction men use it from the start to the finish of every job. Whether they are building a house or a road or a skyscraper, bridging a river or tunneling under it, they must be able to make an exactly measured plan of the work before they begin. They must be able to choose and order materials that are the exact size, weight, and strength that will be needed. They must be able to carry out their plans exactly, too, by giving accurate instructions to the men who work with them. They couldn't do any of these things without using the language of measurement.

Manufacturers also use the language of measurement because they work with materials that have to be measured and put together according to carefully calculated patterns or designs or formulas, and that are sold in carefully measured lots or quantities.

Scientists, of course, couldn't get along without this language because exact measurements are such an important part of their work. In order to perform their research and experiments, and report on them, they must measure all sorts of things with precision — light, heat, time and speed; chemicals and many other substances; electric and atomic power, the force of a hurricane and the thrust of a jet; the size of a tiny microbe and the vast distances between planets and stars.

If the language of measurement were suddenly forgotten, and all the instruments we use for measuring were suddenly lost, no more scientific experiments could be made.

Other important things would come to an end, too, if that happened. Doctors, for example, couldn't give patients the correct doses of medicine. When trains and automobiles and planes broke down, they couldn't be repaired or replaced. In fact it would probably be impossible to keep our modern world operating without the language and the instruments of measurement.

4

Which is heavier — a pound of feathers or a pound of lead?

A Pound of Lead and a
Pound of Feathers

THERE is an old riddle which goes like this: Which is heavier — a
pound of lead or a pound of feathers?

The riddle puzzles some people. They know that lead is very heavy, and that feathers are very light. So they are apt to think the answer must be: a pound of lead is heavier than a pound of feathers.

But everyone who understands the language of measurement knows that the correct answer is: they both weigh the same.

This is the right answer because the word *pound*, the way we use it in our language of measurement, always means exactly one thing. It always stands for a certain amount of weight.

It is true that a piece of lead weighing one pound wouldn't be nearly as big as a bag of feathers weighing one pound. The lead and feathers wouldn't look alike either. They probably wouldn't be the same color. They certainly wouldn't be the same shape. The two things, in other words, would seem to be different in nearly every way.

But a pound of lead and a pound of feathers are alike in at least one way, because they both weigh the same.

A length of ribbon 5,280 feet, or one mile long, is like a mile-long stretch of road in one way, too, because they are both the same length.

And though a bushel of corn may cost only a few cents, and a bushel of diamonds would probably cost millions of dollars, those two things are also alike in one way: they both occupy the same amount of space. Or we could say that they both have the same *volume*, or fill containers of equal *capacity*.

Not Big, Not Little

It is easy to imagine the kind of arguments that would take place every day, if the words in our language of measurement had vague meanings, like the words *big* and *little*. These two words cause arguments all the time.

Suppose you tell a friend that you will meet him in "a little while," and he expects you in five minutes. You arrive at the end of two hours. Five minutes is his idea of a little while. Two hours is yours. That sort of confusion is often the beginning of an argument.

If the word *pound* was as vague as the word *little,* this is the sort of thing that might happen:

You plan a picnic with a friend, and decide that you should take along enough meat to make two hamburgers for each of you. You both agree that you will need a pound. So you go into a store and ask the butcher for a pound of hamburger, take the wrapped package he gives you, and open it only when you have reached your picnic spot. Then you find that the package contains a tiny bit of meat, not even enough to make one hamburger.

When you return home you are hungry, and very angry, and you go straight to the butcher.

"You gave me only a little bit of hamburger," you say. "I asked you for a pound."

The butcher looks surprised. "I gave you what *I* call a pound," he says. "I can't help it if you think a pound of meat is a lot more than what I gave you."

You can see what a lot of trouble would be caused if each person had his own idea of a pound — or of a mile or an inch or a quart, or any of the other words in our language of measurement.

Scales and Yardsticks

A *scale* is the measuring tool we use when we want to weigh something — lead or feathers, meat or candy.

7

There is, for example, the kind of scale you might see at the meat counter of a grocery store. If you tell the butcher that you want a pound of hamburger, he puts some meat on the weighing platform, the flat part of the scale below the dial. Then he adds a little more meat, or takes away a little, until the needle swinging along the dial points right at the big black number 1. That tells both you and the butcher that there is exactly one pound of meat on the scale.

There are many different kinds of scales. Some measure very tiny amounts, one ounce or less. Some measure very heavy objects that weigh many tons.

There is a scale on which a scientist can weigh a particle of material so light that it would take more than half a million of them to weigh an ounce. There is also a scale with a platform so large that a truck can drive right onto it. It is used to measure the loads which trucks carry.

Many grocery stores today have scales which show both the weight and the price of anything that is put on them. You can see such a scale at the vegetable counter of a supermarket. Let's say that you want to buy a head of cabbage, on a day when cabbage is selling for ten cents a pound. You pick out the head you want and the clerk puts it on the scale. The scale tells him that the cabbage weighs a pound and a half, and also tells him that the price of a pound and a half of anything, at ten cents a pound, is fifteen cents.

Yardsticks, foot rules, and *tape measures* are some of the tools we use when we want to measure length. We use them to measure off exactly one inch or one foot or one yard of something — of ribbon, perhaps, or of curtain material, or of lumber.

Yardsticks and foot rules are usually made of wood or plastic or metal. A dressmaker's tape measure is sometimes made of cloth. A carpenter's tape measure is usually a thin strip of steel, coiled

8

like a spring inside a small metal case. The carpenter pulls one end of the tape out of the case when he wants to measure something. When he is finished, he presses a button on the side of the case and the tape measure snaps back into its box. A surveyor's tape measure is made of metal, too.

Whose Foot?

LONG, long ago, in prehistoric times, there were no rulers or yardsticks or other such measuring tools. When men first began to

A "two-foot-long" fish, as measured by early man.

9

measure things, they probably measured by their own fingers or the width of their own palms, or by their own arms or feet.

"This is a three-finger spearhead," a man might say.

Or, "This fish is as long as my foot put down two times."

When a man measured things in that way he was using his finger and his foot just as we use inch and foot markings on a yardstick. When we measure a thing by inches, we are using an inch as our *unit of measurement*. When we measure a thing by feet, we are using a foot as our unit of measurement. Prehistoric man's own finger and foot were some of his units of measurement.

The word *unit* comes from the Latin word that means one. A unit of measurement is any one standard amount, quantity, or value that is used to measure other amounts, quantities, or values.

Prehistoric man probably found his units of measurement very convenient, because they were always with him, wherever he went. But each man's units were a little different from the units other men were using — and that could cause trouble.

A tall man with a very long foot, and a short man with a very short foot, could easily get into an argument when they both measured the same thing by their own feet.

Let's say that a tall man and a short man, hunting together, killed a deer. Each man measured it, using his own foot. Then they cut the animal up and carried home the parts their families liked best to eat. When they got home, people asked them how big the deer had been.

"It was the length of nine feet," the short man said.

But the tall man, whose foot was much longer, said, "Oh, no. It was the length of seven feet."

Let's say they argued about the length of the deer until they got into a real quarrel.

The tall prehistoric man says the deer is seven "feet" long, but the short man says it is nine "feet" long!

Quarrels of that kind were probably the reason why certain chiefs of prehistoric tribes made the world's first laws of measurement.

A chief might have said something like this: "From now on I will allow no man to use his own foot or his own finger or palm or arm for measuring the length of things. From now on all men must measure by my foot, my finger, my palm, and my arm."

A chief who did that was giving his people what are called *standards of measurement.* The word *standard* comes from an old word that means a thing held up, like a signal or a banner. The chief, we might say, held up his own foot and decreed that that particular unit of measurement would be the *standard unit* for all measuring-by-feet from then on.

Probably his people marked off the length of the chief's foot on sticks, and each man carried one of those marked sticks when he wanted to measure something. It would not be as convenient as his own foot, perhaps, but it would prevent quarrels because all the measuring sticks in his tribe would be marked in the same way.

To this day, rulers or governments of most countries of the world set the standards of weights and measures for their people to follow. These *legal standards,* as they are called, are valuable for two reasons.

Legal standards prevent arguments and quarrels over the true length of a foot, the true weight of a pound, and other units of measurement.

Legal standards also protect honest people from dishonest ones. If the weight of a pound, for example, is set by law, a man who charges you for a full pound of meat, and gives you less than a pound, can be punished by law.

Many Feet

PREHISTORIC men didn't have many units of measurement because they didn't measure many kinds of things. And if the standards of measurement were different for each tribe, and they changed with each new chief, it probably didn't matter very much to those wandering hunters of long ago.

But men had to learn new and different ways of measuring things when they began to live in new and different ways.

12

An acre was originally the amount of land a yoke of oxen could plow in one day.

After they learned how to raise cattle and crops, for example, they had to learn how to measure their fields, their herds, and their harvests. Probably a man first measured his farm by finding out how long it took to plow it. The unit of land measurement we use today, an *acre*, was originally the amount of land a yoke of oxen could plow in one day.

After men began to live in towns and cities, they had to learn how to measure still other things — the building materials for their houses and temples and palaces, the cloth they wove, and the wealth of gold and silver they collected.

13

Roman conquerors forcing new subjects to accept their standards of measurement.

One of the earliest units men invented was called the *cubit* — originally the distance from a man's elbow to the tip of his middle finger. This very old unit is even mentioned in the Bible. Noah's Ark, the Bible says, was 300 cubits long, 50 cubits wide, and 30 cubits high.

When a certain city became very powerful and conquered enough other cities to establish a kingdom, the conquerors usually insisted upon everyone accepting their own units and standards of measurement.

The Romans who conquered most of western Europe and parts of Asia and Africa, forced all their new subjects to use the standard they called a *foot*. The Roman foot was a little shorter than the foot we use as a standard unit today — probably because most Romans were not very big men.

The Romans also taught their subjects to use a new unit called a *pace*, for measuring long distances. The Romans invented it so that they could measure the long stone-paved roads they built to connect all the parts of their great empire with their capital city, Rome. The pace was the distance from the heel of one foot to the heel of the same foot when it next touched the ground, or about five of our feet. A thousand of these double steps, or paces, made up the much bigger unit which the Romans called a *milia passuum*, or a thousand paces. Their word *milia*, for thousand, gives us our word, mile.

After the Roman Empire broke up, most people in Europe continued to measure things in feet and miles, but they no longer all used the same standards.

In England, for example, sometime before the tenth century, the foot had become a unit more than 13 of our inches long, and the mile had become a unit of about 6,600 feet. In other parts of

15

Europe, the mile came to have a length as short as 3,300 feet and as long as 36,000 feet, or nearly seven times as long as our mile today, 5,280 feet.

Differences in units and standards of measurements between one part of the world and another often made it difficult for people to buy and sell goods back and forth across boundary lines. An English merchant of the fourteenth or fifteenth century, who measured cloth in English yards, had trouble when he wanted to order a certain amount of cloth from, say, a weaver in India who measured things by the unit he called a *hath* — a unit about 18 inches long.

But most people preferred to keep their own units, only because they were used to them, even if the units were different from those used in other lands.

Also, most people in those early days weren't in the habit of noticing whether the piece of cloth or length of rope they bought had been measured with absolute accuracy according to their own units. Although rulers, yardsticks, and other measuring instruments existed by that time, they were often carelessly made and didn't match the standard units decreed by various kings.

Then, about the time Columbus discovered America, over four hundred and fifty years ago, a new age of science began. For the first time, many men in many lands wanted to measure all sorts of things with absolute accuracy. They also wanted to write and talk to each other about the new things they were discovering and the new experiments they were making. Those first scientists of our modern world were not satisfied with the methods of measurement they had to use. They knew they couldn't make progress until all scientists everywhere could make accurate measurements, and talk and write to each other in a language of measurement they could all understand.

16

The fourteenth-century Englishman measured cloth in yards but the Indian merchant measured it in haths.

In the seventeenth century a French astronomer, Jean Picard, suggested that scientists themselves should work out a new system of measurement that everybody could use — quickly, easily, and accurately. In 1790 the French National Assembly appointed a committee to decide on the units that would be used in such a system. The system that committee invented is known today as the *metric system.*

Eyes, Wrelbows and Smiths

ALMOST anyone can invent units of measurement. Let's say you decide to invent some yourself, for measuring length.

You decide that the width of your eye would be a useful unit for measuring small things. You call this unit an *eye.*

Then, for measuring larger things, you invent a larger unit — the distance from your elbow to your wrist. You name this unit by putting together the word elbow and part of the word for wrist. You call it a *wrelbow.*

For measuring still larger things you invent an even larger unit — your own height. You call this unit a *smith,* because your name is Smith.

To make your units more useful, let's say you figure out how they are related to each other — how many eyes are in a wrelbow, and how many wrelbows are in a smith. You discover, by measuring one against the other, that there are 9 eyes in a wrelbow, and 7 wrelbows in a smith.

Now you have what could be called a whole *system of measurement.* You have done what men did, long ago, when they figured out how the length of a foot was related to a smaller unit that was probably originally the width of a thumb — the unit that became

18

our inch. When we say today that there are 12 inches in a foot, we are using a very old system of measurement. That system has been in existence ever since certain men first agreed that there were 12 thumb-widths, or inches, in a foot. (Later on, in England, when the king decreed that an inch would be the length of three dry barleycorns laid in a row, the system did not change. Twelve of those barleycorn inches were still called a foot.)

You could make a measuring instrument too, a tool for using your new system. It might be a wooden stick one smith long, which you call a *smithstick*. You could mark the smith off into 7 wrelbows, and mark each wrelbow off into 9 eyes. With this smithstick you could measure all sorts of things by the units of your new system.

You might measure a desk and learn that it was 2 wrelbows and 3 eyes wide. You might measure a boat and learn that it was exactly 2 smiths long. You would discover that it is quite easy and satisfactory to use your new system of measurement.

But soon you would discover something else, too. If you told a friend that your boat was 2 smiths long, he wouldn't know what you meant. If you went into a store and asked for 7 smiths of fish-line, the clerk wouldn't know what you meant either. Eventually, you would discover that nobody knew what you meant when you talked about your new units of measurement. You would be using a language of measurement people didn't understand.

Perhaps you might try to convince everyone else to measure things by eyes, wrelbows, and smiths, so that they too could speak your language of measurement. But if you did that probably no one, not even your best friend, would listen to you. They would probably say that your new units were no better or easier to use than inches, feet, and yards. And they would also tell you that they preferred to go on using the units they already knew, and to speak the language of measurement they already understood.

There are only two ways to persuade people to use units that are new and strange to them. One way is by the decree of a king or a government. When the Romans conquered most of Europe, for example, their new subjects began to measure things by the Roman foot because the Roman rulers ordered them to.

The other way is to convince people that the strange new units are much better than the units they have been using. When the members of the French National Assembly Committee went to work to figure out a new system of measurement in 1790, they made up their minds that their new system would be better than all the systems of measurement the world had ever known. They reasoned that everyone would be glad to use this new and better system so that everyone would speak the same language of measurement.

The First Universal Unit: The Meter

THE first thing those French scientists did when they started work on their new system of measurement was to decide that they should invent a completely new unit for measuring length. This unit, they said, would be the basis, or foundation, of their whole system.

They agreed that the new unit should be something as natural and familiar as a man's foot, because people were in the habit of using that kind of unit. They also agreed that this unit should not really be a man's foot, or anything else that might be longer or shorter in one part of the world than another, or that might change as time went by. They wanted a unit that never changed, that would always be exactly the same at all times and all places.

Certain of these scientists said, "We can find the clue to our new

20

French scientists planning the metric system.

unit in the size of the earth. Take a circle running around the earth through the North and South Poles — one of the imaginary lines we call meridians. Divide the circle into four equal parts. And then divide one of those quarter-circles, say the part going from the equator to the North Pole, into ten million equal parts. One of those ten million parts could be our new unit. We could call it a *meter*, from the ancient Greek word that means measure."

Gradually more and more scientists agreed that the meter would be a satisfactory unit of measurement for accurate scientific work. And finally it was decided that this unit, 39.3701 inches long, should be the basis for their whole new system of measurement which they named the *metric system*.

The Metric System

THE most important thing to remember about the metric system is this: the meter is the only *natural unit* in the whole system. All other units are based on the meter, and can be figured out by anyone who knows how long a meter is.

All the units smaller than one meter in this system can be figured out by dividing one meter into parts — into 10 parts, or 100 parts, or 1,000 parts, or 1,000,000 parts, or even ten-times-1,000,000 parts.

All the units larger than one meter in this system can be figured out just as easily, by multiplying the meter by 10, or by 100, or by 1,000, or by 1,000,000 and so on.

The metric system is sometimes called a *decimal system*, from the Latin word *decem*, for ten, because each unit is either 10 times larger or 10 times smaller than the unit next to it in size. Like all decimal systems, it is easy for most people to use, because most people would rather divide and multiply by 10 than by numbers such as 12 (the number of inches in our foot) or 36 (the number of inches in our yard).

The scientists who invented the metric system also assigned names for all the units in the system. Each name was devised by putting part of a Greek or Latin word in front of the word meter.

The names of all the units smaller than the meter were constructed with the help of Latin words. One-tenth of a meter, for example, is called a *decimeter*, from the Latin word for ten. The next smaller unit, one-hundredth of a meter, is called a *centimeter*, from the Latin word *centum*, meaning one hundred.

The names of all units larger than the meter were constructed with the help of Greek words. The unit ten times larger than the meter, for example, is called a *decameter*, from the Greek prefix *deka*, meaning ten. The unit one hundred times larger than a meter is called a *hectometer*, from the Greek word for hundred. The unit 1,000 times larger than a meter is called a *kilometer*, from the Greek word for 1,000. There are about 3,300 feet in a kilometer. It takes about 1 3/5 kilometers to make one of our miles.

The scientists who invented the metric system for measuring length showed that it could also be used for measuring weight.

They invented a unit of weight called a *gram*. It was the weight of a cube of pure water at a fixed temperature measuring 1 centimeter, or one-hundredth of a meter, in each direction. Since water, like everything else, weighs more at sea level than at higher altitudes, the scientists were careful to say that the standard unit of the gram would be the weight of one cubic centimeter of water at sea level.

Dividing or multiplying the gram by 10, over and over again, gave the scientists units 10 times, 100 times, and 1,000 times smaller or larger than a gram. A kilogram, sometimes called a

"Milestones" are still in use throughout the world; this French one gives the distance to a town in kilometers.

"kilo," is 1,000 grams. A kilo is a little more than two of our pounds.

Scientists, of course, were the first to adopt the metric system. They preferred it because it was easy to use and because it was so accurate. Today, in every civilized land, the language of the metric system is the language of measurement used by scientists.

The metric system also became the legal system of measurement in France soon after the American Revolution. During the next century it became the legal system in other European countries too, and in the lands of South America.

24

In all those places people began to buy their cloth by the meter, and their fruits and vegetables by the kilogram. And when they bought things that had to be measured in containers — such as milk — these containers were made according to the new metric system for measuring volume or capacity. The most important metric unit of capacity is called a *liter*. A liter fills a container the shape of a cube which measures ten centimeters on each side, or one cubic decimeter.

But the metric system did not immediately become the legal system of measurement all over the world, as we shall see.

Where Our Standards Come From

BEFORE the American Revolution, when America was an English colony, Americans used the standards of weights and measures decreed by English kings — just as they used the English coins called pence, shillings, and pounds.

The units of measurement those early Americans used had names that are still familiar to us today — inches, feet and yards, ounces, pounds and tons, pints, quarts and gallons.

But when Americans won their freedom, and began to govern themselves, they gave their new United States Congress the power to regulate the value of the country's coins, and to fix the standards of the weights and measures.

Thomas Jefferson, who was a member of Congress in its early years, persuaded the other members to issue new United States coins according to a decimal system based on the unit we call a *dollar*. Among the new coins was a *dime*, which was one-tenth of a dollar, and a *cent*, which was one-tenth of a dime or one-hundredth of a dollar. Our word dime comes from the Latin word *decem*, for ten. Our word cent comes from the Latin word *centum*, for hundred.

Thomas Jefferson and many other men interested in science, wanted Congress to adopt a decimal system of weights and measures, too. But Congress decided, after a delay of many years, to adopt instead the system Americans already knew and used — the English system. And when Congress asked for copies of the English government's official standards of weights and measures,

Thomas Jefferson persuading Congress to adopt the decimal system based on the dollar.

copies of those standards were made and sent to the United States. One was a metal weight that weighed exactly one English pound. The other was a metal bar marked off to show exactly one English yard.

That weight and that bar became the legal standards of weight and measure for our country. They were used for checking the accuracy of scales, yardsticks, and all sorts of other measuring instruments all over the United States.

But after the metric system became legal throughout a large part of the world, scientists and many other people urged Congress to make it the legal system in the United States too. And finally, in 1866, Congress passed a law which said that Americans could go on using the old English system if they wished, but that the metric system was also legal in the United States.

A few years later the United States agreed to help support an International Bureau of Weights and Measures, set up in France in a palace near Paris. In that Bureau, for years, were kept the world's official metric standards — a cylinder made of platinum and iridium, weighing exactly one kilogram, and a platinum and iridium bar marked to show exactly the length of one meter.

Exact copies of those standards were sent to any country that wanted to use them as its own standards. Copies were sent to China where for centuries people had bought their rice by the *chin*, which was about 1 1/3 pounds. In 1929 when China received its new metric standards, people began to buy their rice by a new weight called the *kung chin*, which was about 2 2/10 pounds, or exactly one kilogram.

The United States received its own copies of those standards too. They were kept under glass in a sealed vault, in our own Bureau of Standards in Washington, D.C. If they had to be

Standard weights and measures are kept under glass where no human hands can touch them.

moved, they were handled very carefully with metal tongs. The air around them was always at the same temperature and the same humidity. They were treated with such care in the hope that nothing would happen to them that would change their size or weight to even the smallest degree. They were the standards used for checking the accuracy of measuring tools made and used in our country.

But present-day scientists can measure with more accuracy than men could measure two centuries ago, when the metric system was being invented. And modern industry demands measurements more exact than any ever needed before.

That is why twentieth-century experts decided that a meter standard made of metal was no longer good enough. They knew it might change very slightly, or that it might be lost or stolen. And they had discovered that measurements made with the help of that meter bar might be inaccurate to as much as one ten-millionth of a meter. A mistake even that tiny could be very serious to an astronomer, for example, or to a scientist making the devices to guide a satellite in a certain orbit.

So in 1960 experts from all over the world met at Paris to decide on a new and still more accurate standard for the meter. The new one they chose is based on the wave length of a particular kind of light — the orange-red light given off by a rare gas called krypton.

Today the standard meter of the world is 1,650,763.73 wave lengths of that light. Scientists use this new standard with the help of a measuring tool called an interferometer, which counts wave lengths and tiny fractions of wave lengths.

Today in the United States the two systems — the old English one and the metric system — are both still legal. But today if you ask one of the experts at the National Bureau of Standards to tell you the length of a yard, he will not answer, "Three feet, or thirty-six inches." Instead he will say, "The yard is 914/1,000, or about 9/10 of a meter, and a meter is 1,650,763.73 wave lengths of krypton."

Perhaps some day the metric system will be the *only* legal system of measurement used in the United States. If that happens, businessmen will have to change thousands of measuring tools, redraw thousands of plans, and reset devices on thousands of machines. But American scientists will probably be very pleased. Then they will use one measuring system all the time — in their work and in their home life too.

Measuring Temperature

In the United States today we also use two systems for measuring temperature. One is called *Fahrenheit,* and the other *centigrade.* Each system uses a unit called a degree, but Fahrenheit degrees do not mean the same as centigrade degrees.

The system most used in our country, except by scientists, is the Fahrenheit system, named for Gabriel Daniel Fahrenheit who invented it about 250 years ago. By this system the freezing point of water is 32° above the zero point on the scale and its boiling point 212°. Most of the thermometers that we use in our daily life are Fahrenheit thermometers. That is, they measure temperature by the Fahrenheit system, in Fahrenheit degrees.

30

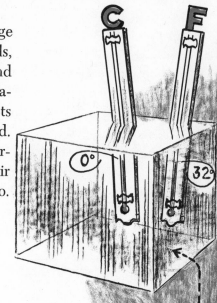

The Centigrade and Fahrenheit systems of measuring temperature.

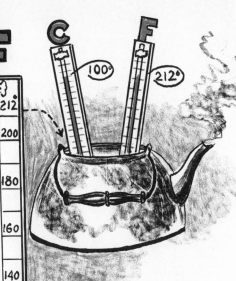

On a very hot day, when someone tells you that the temperature has gone up to "90," he means that the Fahrenheit thermometer reads 90 degrees. On a cold day, when someone tells you that the temperature has gone down to freezing, he means that the Fahrenheit thermometer reads 32 degrees.

By the centigrade system the freezing point of water is zero degrees, and the boiling point is 100 degrees. Because there are 100 degrees between these points, the centigrade system was named for the Latin word *centum*, meaning hundred. It is also called the *Celsius thermometer* after Anders Celsius, a Swedish astronomer, who first invented it.

Most scientists prefer to use the centigrade system, just as they prefer to use the metric system for measuring length, weight, and capacity.

People who use thermometers a great deal usually use a small circle (°) to stand for the word degree. They also use the letters F. and C. to stand for Fahrenheit and centigrade. They always show by one of these letters which of the two systems of measurement they are using.

The freezing point of water, for example, would be written 0° C. in the centigrade system, and 32° F. in

31

the Fahrenheit system. If you put a centigrade thermometer into a pot of boiling water, you could write down the temperature of the water like this: 100° C. If you put a Fahrenheit thermometer into the same pot, you would write it as 212° F. (Of course, the pot of boiling water must be at sea level to get these readings, because the boiling point of water is 100° C. or 212° F. only at sea level. At higher altitudes water boils at lower temperatures.)

If you want to indicate a temperature reading below the freezing point of water you put a minus sign (–) before the number like this: –10° F. or –2° C.

A Weights and Measures Inspector at Work

THIS is Mr. Green, a weights and measures inspector for the State of New York. Every morning he sets out in his car with all the things he will need for testing the scales, yardsticks, and other measuring tools used by business people in the territory he covers. All the equipment he carries with him — his own scales and other measuring instruments — have been carefully checked for accuracy in the State capitol, which has its own copies of the national standards in Washington.

Today Mr. Green goes first to a big supermarket. He knows most of the clerks there, because he visits the store at least four times a year. But, since he never announces his visits ahead of time, none of the clerks knew Mr. Green would arrive today.

First he tests each scale, to make sure it weighs things accurately. He then marks each accurate scale with a green seal. This is called *sealing* the scale.

When a housewife sees this green seal on the scale at a food counter, she knows that the food she buys at the counter will weigh exactly what the scale tells her it weighs, and that the scale is accurate.

If Mr. Green finds a scale that is not accurate, he marks it with a big red tag. He doesn't have to use a red tag very often, but he uses one today. When he puts the standard pound weight he carries with him on the supermarket's vegetable scale, he finds that the scale reads on ounce over a pound. So he ties one of his red tags to the scale. In big black letters on the tag are the words:
CONDEMNED UNTIL REPAIRED AND SEALED.

When a weights and measures inspector finds a scale inaccurate, he marks it with a red tag.

The manager of the store is upset when he sees the tag. He did not know that the scale was out of order. He removes it immediately from the vegetable counter, and sends it away to be readjusted. He will not use it again until Mr. Green has tested it once more and sealed it with a green seal. The manager knows that if he tries to use the scale before it has been repaired and tested again, he will be breaking the law and may be arrested.

Before Mr. Green leaves the supermarket, he also tests the weight of many ready-packaged foods. He picks up a package of pork chops marked 1 lb. 12 oz., and weighs it to make sure it really weighs exactly one pound and twelve ounces. He tests many other packages of meat, too, and some samples of the store's packaged cheese and vegetables.

Mr. Green has so much work to do in the supermarket that he spends the whole morning there.

In the afternoon he stops a traveling fish merchant he meets on the road, and tests his scale. He also visits several gasoline stations. At each station he tests the pumps, to make sure they measure gas accurately as they pump it into the fuel tanks of cars and trucks.

Some of the other places that Mr. Green visits several times each year are drugstores, department stores, dairies, coalyards, and packing plants where farm products are weighed and packaged for sale.

When he tests the scales used by a dealer in jewelry or precious metals, Mr. Green uses his set of weights called *troy weights*. These are different from the weights called *avoirdupois* weights, which he uses for ordinary commodities. A troy ounce is a little heavier than the more common avoirdupois ounce, and in the troy pound there are only 12 ounces instead of the 16 ounces in the avoirdupois pound.

34

A weights and measures inspector checking the accuracy of a gasoline pump.

When Mr. Green tests the scales used by a druggist he uses another special set of weights called *apothecaries' weights*. (Apothecary is an old word for druggist.) These are very tiny weights based on the troy ounce. In the system of apothecaries' weights there are 8 drams to an ounce, 3 scruples in a dram, and 20 grains in a scruple.

When Mr. Green tests a department store's yardsticks, he uses a standard yardstick he carries with him. He also makes sure that the store's yardsticks have sturdy metal strips at each end so that the wood cannot break off or wear away. He tests a store's cloth-measuring machine by running through it the strip of cloth he carries with him. It is very sturdy cloth which doesn't shrink or stretch, and which is marked off in inches and yards.

At a dairy he tests the bottle-filling machines by using his own standard containers which have capacities of exactly one quart, one pint, and one-half pint.

Mr. Green doesn't test the scales people use in their own homes to weigh themselves on. He doesn't test a housewife's tape measure, or the foot rule a man uses when he builds a set of bookshelves. The only instruments Mr. Green tests are those used to weigh and measure goods that will be sold.

In almost every state in our country there are men like Mr. Green at work. All of them do not use green seals to show that a scale is accurate. Some use seals of other colors. But whenever they put a seal on an instrument of measurement, people can be sure that the instrument is accurate.

Like other inspectors who work for the federal government, and who check the weight of the contents of canned goods, for example, these state inspectors of weights and measures have just one job: to protect the public.

On Time

OUR system of measuring time in units called *seconds, minutes,* and *hours,* is very old. It has been used in most of the civilized countries of the world for many centuries.

In France, about two hundred years ago, people did experiment for a while with a decimal system for measuring time. They divided each day into 10 hours, each hour into 100 minutes, and each minute into 100 seconds. But the decimal system of measuring time was never popular, and people quickly gave it up.

Today in France, as in all the rest of the civilized world, people divide each day into 24 hours, each hour into 60 minutes, and each minute into 60 seconds.

Clocks and watches are the most common tools we use for measuring time. These accurate modern instruments take the place of ancient time-measuring devices, such as the sundial, the hourglass with its trickling sand, or various kinds of water clocks. You probably look at a clock or a watch very often every day, so that you will get up on time, get to school on time, get to a meeting on time, or get home on time.

Probably, too, you check your clock regularly with the time signals sent out each day by the National Bureau of Standards, through local radio and TV stations. You know that if the clock in your house is slow, you may miss a bus or arrive at a party when it is half over. You know that if your clock is fast, you may wait many minutes for a friend to meet you before he finally arrives. Everybody wants clocks and watches that tell the truth — that is, measure time accurately.

Of course the correct time for one part of the world is not the correct time for every other part. As our earth spins around, rotating always toward the east, the sun appears above New York, for example, three hours before it appears above San Francisco. High noon in New York, therefore, occurs three hours earlier than high noon in San Francisco.

If each person set his own clock at noon every day, at the very moment when the sun was highest over his own head, there would be thousands of different times in the world. The clocks in your

Clocks have taken the place of early measuring devices such as sundials, hourglasses and marked-off candles.

own town probably wouldn't read exactly the same as the clocks in a town only a few miles away. Every time you went to another town, to shop or to see a movie, you would have to remember that the clocks in that town might read differently from your own. If you traveled in an airplane from New York to San Francisco, you would have to keep changing your watch all the time.

Before the days of trains, the clocks in each part of the world were set according to the sun at that particular place. But in those days people didn't travel very much, and if they did, they traveled slowly, by sailing ship or horseback. If a man finally reached a town some distance from his home, he didn't mind having to change his timepiece to suit the time of that place.

But after the invention of trains, more people began to travel about the world, and they traveled more swiftly. Then the differ-

Differences in time caused confusion when people traveled faster by train.

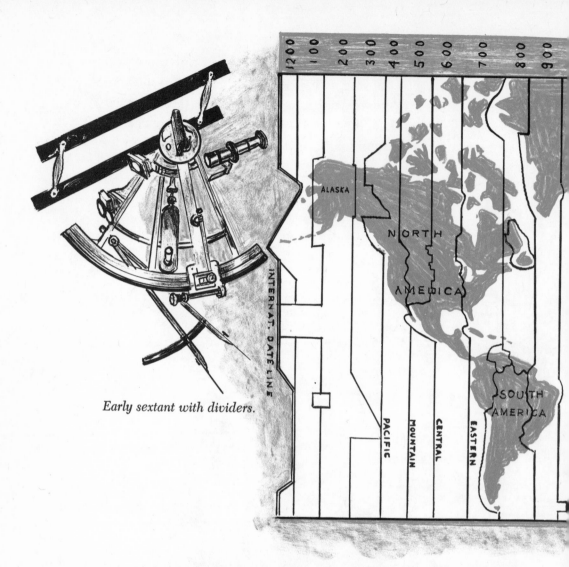

Early sextant with dividers.

The Greenwich Standard Time Zone System. Greenwich Observatory itself lies on the Zero (0) Meridian. Greenwich time is here shown at noon, with clocks east (right) of it each an hour later, and those west (left) each an hour earlier. The four Greenwich time zones running through the United States proper are indicated below North America.

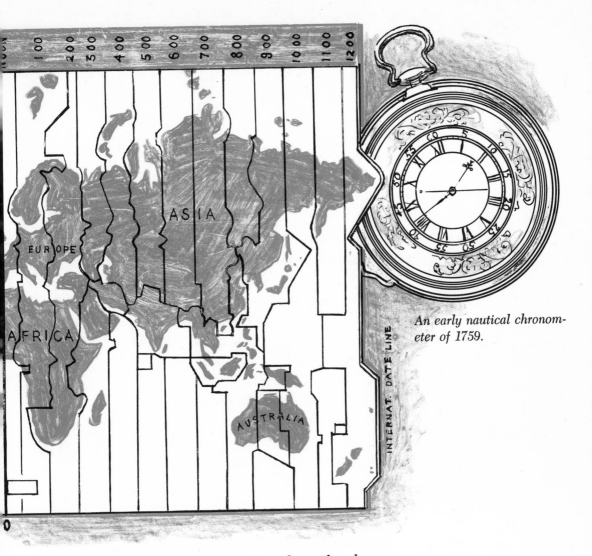

An early nautical chronometer of 1759.

ences in time between one town and another became very confusing. The men who ran the railroads were especially confused. They didn't know how to make out their timetables.

"This train is going from New York to Smithville," they might have said. "It will leave New York at noon, and it will arrive in

Smithville nine hours later. According to New York time it will arrive in Smithville at 9 o'clock. But according to Smithville time, it will arrive there at 8:15. Which hour — 9 or 8:15 — shall we put on the timetable?"

In the year 1884, scientists from nearly every part of the world met together at Washington, D.C., to try to bring some order into the confusion of the world's clocks. They decided to divide the world into 24 numbered segments, or time zones, each running from the North Pole to the South Pole. Each time zone, they decided, would have its own time.

The Number One Zone runs along the Zero Meridian, sometimes called the Greenwich Meridian in honor of the famous Observatory in the town of Greenwich, England. Greenwich is on that meridian. The time kept in this zone, usually called the Greenwich Zone, is now the standard time for the whole world because all the other zones take their time from it.

The first zone east of Greenwich keeps its clocks an hour later than Greenwich Standard Time. The next zone to the east keeps its clocks two hours later than Greenwich Standard Time, and so on through twelve of the zones. The zones west of Greenwich keep their clocks one or two or more hours earlier than Greenwich Standard Time, depending on the number of the zone.

The map shows the four time zones that run through the United States. It explains why the clocks of New York keep what is called Eastern Time, and the clocks of San Francisco keep what is called Pacific Time. Eastern Time is 5 hours earlier than Greenwich Standard Time. Pacific Time is 8 hours earlier than Greenwich Standard Time.

These time zones make it easy for railroadmen to prepare their timetables. If a train leaves New York at 12 noon E.S.T. (Eastern Standard Time), and arrives nine hours later in Smithville, its

42

arrival time is 9 P.M. E.S.T., if Smithville is also in the Eastern time zone. If Smithville is in the next zone to the west, where the time is one hour earlier, the arrival time is 8 P.M. C.S.T., or 8 P.M. Central Standard Time. In the summer, of course, when clocks are set ahead an hour to Daylight Saving Time, the timetables change too. Then a timetable might say that a train leaves New York at 12 noon E.D.T. (Eastern Daylight Time), and arrives in Smithville at 8 P.M. C.D.T. (Central Daylight Time).

If you fly west across the United States today, from New York to San Francisco, you don't have to keep changing your watch all the time. You just move it back one hour each time you cross from one time zone into the next. If you fly east across the United States, from California to New York, you move your watch ahead one hour each time you cross into another time zone.

Modern ships all carry two clocks, one set always to Greenwich Standard Time, the other set at noon each day at the moment when the sun is highest overhead. The difference in time between his two clocks tells a ship's captain how far west or east of Greenwich he is.

Calendars for Today and Yesterday

CALENDARS measure time too. The word calendar comes from a Latin word meaning an account book. A calendar is an account of time. The calendars we use most often in our everyday life measure time in units of days, weeks, months, and years.

In our calendar, years are numbered beginning with the traditional date of the birth of Jesus Christ. Our calendar, in other words, measures the duration of the Christian Era. That's why

A calendar keeps an account of time in days, weeks, months, and years.

we sometimes write a date like this: A.D. 1945. The letters, A.D., stand for the Latin words, *anno Domini*, which mean "in the year of (our) Lord." When we want to talk about something that happened before the birth of Christ, we use the letters B.C., which stand for the words "before Christ." We might say, for example, that an Egyptian pyramid was built in the year 1000 B.C.

The calendar we use is not the only one in the world. Arabs use a calendar which measures the length of the Mohammedan Era, beginning in the year A.D. 622, when the prophet Mohammed started to preach his new religion. In the Arabs' calendar the year 1 is our year 622.

The Hebrew calendar begins 3,760 years B.C. at the time when — people once thought — the world was created. A Hebrew year is not quite as long as a year on our calendar.

Until quite recently nobody could learn the age of things which existed on the earth before there were any calendars at all — that is, in prehistoric times. But scientists can now measure the age of ancient things which contain certain radioactive substances, such as a kind of carbon called *Carbon 14*. By measuring the amount of Carbon 14 in a prehistoric mammoth bone, for example, scientists can find out how many thousands of years ago that animal lived.

Special Tools for Measuring

THE tape measure you use for measuring a room can also be used for measuring all sorts of other things — a piece of cloth, for example, or a fishing line. The scale on which a butcher weighs meat can also be used to weigh candy or vegetables.

But certain things must always be measured by instruments made especially for that purpose. Many of these instruments are called *meters,* from the Greek word for measure which gave us the name of the basic unit of the metric system.

The amount of gas or electricity used in your house is measured by a *gas meter* or an *electric meter*. The company which supplies the gas or the electric current sends a man to "read" the meters every month or two. By reading the figures on the meter dials, he can learn how much gas or electricity has been used in your house since his previous visit.

The water pumped into a house from a city water supply is measured by a *water meter.*

By reading the figures on the meter dials, this man can tell how much electricity the owners of the house have used.

A photographer uses a *light meter* to measure the amount of light illuminating the scene or person he wants to photograph.

The names of other special measuring instruments have been made by putting the word meter together with another word. A *speedometer*, for example, is the name of an instrument that measures the speed of a car.

An *altimeter* measures the height at which an airplane is flying.

A *tachometer*, also used on airplanes and on some boats and cars too, measures an engine's revolutions per minute, usually written as rpm's. The first part of the instrument's name comes from the Greek word *tachos*, which means swiftness.

A *chronometer* (*chronos* is the Greek word for time) is a special and very accurate kind of clock used on ships.

A *barometer*, from the Greek word *baros*, meaning weight, is an instrument for measuring the pressure (or weight) of the earth's atmosphere. Weather forecasters use barometers to help them foretell weather changes. They also use *anemometers*, which measure the force, or speed of wind. The first part of this instrument's name comes from *anemos*, the Greek word for wind.

A *Fathometer* is used to measure the distance from the surface of a body of water to the bottom, or perhaps to a school of fish hidden in the depths. A *fathom* is a measure of length containing six feet. Originally a fathom was the distance between a man's fingertips, when his arms were extended sideways.

Not all measuring instruments are named using the term meter. A *tire gauge*, for example, is the instrument used to measure the air pressure in bicycle, automobile, and airplane landing-gear tires. The special speedometer in an airplane is called an *air speed indicator*, and the tilt or angle of a plane is measured by its *bank indicator*.

47

An anemometer *is useful for measuring the wind's speed.*

The sensitive device called a *Geiger counter* detects and measures atomic radiation. It is widely used for measuring dangerous radioactive elements.

A Picture Language of Measurement

SOMETIMES measurements can be described better, or more quickly, with a picture than with words. This kind of picture is called a *graph*, or a chart.

If you wanted to know the height of all the students in your class, you might measure them all and say, "Of the twenty-four students in the class, twelve are under 5 feet tall, six are just 5 feet in height, and six are over 5 feet." But if you drew a circle and marked it into sections, one section for each group of students, you could give the information about their height more quickly.

Your circle would look like this:

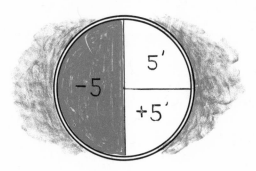

The half-circle marked minus (−) 5′ shows that half of the 24 students in the class are under 5 feet in height. (The sign ′ is often used as an abbreviation for the word feet; the sign ″ is often used as an abbreviation for the word inches.) The other sections show that one-quarter of the class is just 5′ in height and the remaining quarter is over 5′ in height, or plus (+) 5′.

A graph like this is called a *pie-chart*, because it looks like a pie cut into several pieces.

Another kind of graph often used in the same way is called a *bar chart*, because it looks like a row of bars. This is how you could report the height of twenty-four students with a bar chart:

The many different kinds of measurements made in modern science, modern business, and modern government are often indicated on charts or graphs. They are a kind of picture-language of measurement.

New Words in the Language of Measurement

THE language of measurement keeps changing all the time, as our way of life changes.

Many types of charts and graphs are used in modern business offices.

A printer composing a "stick" of hand-set type. Height of type is measured in points — units of 1/72 of an inch.

52

When printing came widely into use, new units were invented for the measuring of type, and the names of those units became a part of our language. Printers measure the size of type by a unit called a *point*, which is about 1/72 of an inch. Twelve points, or nearly 1/6 of an inch, make up a larger unit called a *pica*, usually used to measure the width of a line of type. This book is set in 12-point type and the *measure* of a full line of type on this page is 28 picas.

The word *horsepower* was added to the language of measurement about two hundred years ago by a Scottish inventor, James Watt, who made the world's first widely-used steam engine. Watt's engine could do a great deal of work which, up to that time, had to be done by men or animals. Watt's steam engine could pull a heavy load or lift a heavy weight. At first, however, Watt couldn't tell people exactly how powerful his engine was because in those days there were no units for measuring power.

Watt decided to find out how much work one strong horse could do in one minute, and to call that unit of work, or power, one *horsepower*. With that unit he could measure the work that his steam engine could do.

He harnessed a strong horse to a rope, passed the rope through a series of pulleys, and fastened the other end of the rope to a weight. Then he drove the horse forward, so that the weight was lifted. Watt discovered that the horse could lift a 3,300 pound weight 10 feet into the air in 1 minute.

When Watt tested one of his steam engines he found that in one minute it could lift a 3,300 pound weight 100 feet into the air, or ten times as high as the horse lifted it in the same time. He called that engine a 10-horsepower engine, because it could do ten times as much work as the horse.

How James Watt determined the unit of work called a horsepower.

Today we get power not only from steam engines, but also from gasoline engines, diesel engines, steam and water turbines, electric motors, and atomic reactors. But the unit Watt invented is still part of our language of measurement.

Other new units for measuring power have been invented since the time of James Watt. One was named in his honor. When we talk about 60-watt light bulbs, or 100-watt light bulbs, we are using Watt's name to designate a unit of electric power. Other units for measuring electricity, the *volt* and the *ampere*, were also named for scientists. Alessandro Volta was an Italian physicist; André M. Ampère was a French physicist. The wattmeter, voltmeter and ammeter are the names of the instruments used to measure watts, volts, and amperes.

Another new word came into our language of measurement after scientists had developed telescopes through which men could see objects many millions of miles away from the earth. Those scientists invented a new unit for measuring distances greater than men had even imagined before. They knew that light travels through space at the rate of 186,000 miles each second. At that rate, in the period of a year, a light ray could travel about 6,000,000,000,000 (6 million million, or 6 trillion) miles. This distance is called a *light year*, and is the unit modern astronomers use for measuring the distance between the earth, for example, and a distant star.

The star Sirius is almost 9 light years away from our own solar system.

Two words often seen in newspapers today, *kiloton* and *megaton*, are the names of two new units invented to measure the high-energy liberation (or blasting power) of nuclear bombs. A kiloton

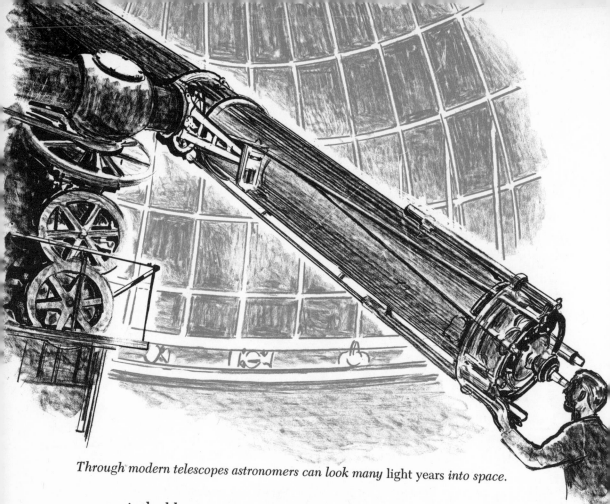

Through modern telescopes astronomers can look many light years into space.

is the blasting power of a thousand tons of TNT (an ordinary high explosive). A megaton is a thousand kilotons, or the blasting power of a million tons of TNT.

Probably in the future, new units of measurement will be invented — units that scientists and others will need as they invent new things and new ways of life. Doubtless, new instruments of measurement will be needed for some of these units. And each new unit, and perhaps each new instrument, too, will add additional words to our language of measurement.

56

Index